DOCUMENTING THE
WAR OF 1812

FAMOUS PEOPLE OF THE WAR OF 1812

Robin Johnson

Crabtree Publishing Company

www.crabtreebooks.com

DOCUMENTING THE WAR OF 1812

Author: Robin Johnson
Editor-in-Chief: Lionel Bender
Editor: Simon Adams
**Publishing plan research
   and development:**
   Sean Charlebois, Reagan Miller
   Crabtree Publishing Company
Project Coordinator:
   Kathy Middleton
Print coordinator:
   Katherine Berti
Photo research: Bridget Heos
Designer and Makeup: Ben White
**Production coordinator
   and prepress technician:**
   Margaret Amy Salter
Production: Kim Richardson
Consultants:
   Richard Jensen, Research Professor
   of History, Culver Stockton
   College, Missouri

   Ronald J. Dale,
   War of 1812 Historian,
   1812 Bicentennial Project Manager,
   Parks Canada

Maps: Stefan Chabluk

Photo credits
Alamy: 12, 21, 38l (North Wind Picture Archives), 16 (P.Spiro), 18 (Ivy Close Images), 33 (Universal Images Group Limited)
Image courtesy of antiqueprints.com: page 19t
Major-General Sir Isaac Brock, KB [President and Administrator of Upper Canada, 1811-12] by George T. Berthon. 694158. Government of Ontario Art Collection, Archives of Ontario: cover (left)
Archives Charmet/The Bridgeman Art Library: 22–23b
The Granger Collection, NYC: 26b
Library of Congress: 1 (LC-USZC2-2800), 4 (LC-DIG-ppmsca-10754), 10l (LC-USZC4-2103), 10r (LC-USZC2-3178), 11b (LC-USZC4-1581), 13 (LC-USZC4-6506), 14t (LC-DIG-ppmsca-24329), 14b (LC-H22-D- 5621), 20–21 (LC-DIG-ppmsca-23121), 21t (LC-DIG-pga-03353), 24–25 (LC-DIG-ppmsca-23089), 25 (LC-USZ62-121124), 27 (LC-USZ61-313), 27–28 (LC-DIG-ppmsca-2309), 29 (LC-DIG-hec-07971), 30b (LC-DIG-pga-02821), 30t (LC-DIG-ppmsca-19923), 32–33 (LC-USZC4-6294), 31b (LC-DIG-ppmsca-23757), 31t (LC-DIG-pga-02909), 35t (LC-USZC4-6776), 34t (LC-USZ62-7431), 38r (LC-DIG-ppmsca-31279), 39–40 (LC-DIG-pga-01011), 41 (LC-USZ62-62)
© North Wind / North Wind Picture Archives: cover (right)
shutterstock.com: 3 (Wally Stemberger), 19b, 36–37
Topfoto (The Granger Collection): 5, 8, 9, 11t, 15, 17r, 35b, 34r, 36t, 37t, 40t
Wikimedia Commons: cover (center); Joseph Brant by Gilbert Stuart (1755–1828): 17l; Harfang: 22t; Southern Methodist University Digital Collections: 26t; U.S. National Archives and Records Administration: 29b

Cover: Three charismatic leaders of the War of 1812: British General (Sir) Isaac Brock, U.S. General (and later, President) Andrew Jackson, and Shawnee Chief Tecumseh.

Title page: U.S. Major-General Winfield Scott reviewing his troops. Currier & Ives c1846.

Library and Archives Canada Cataloguing in Publication

Johnson, Robin (Robin R.)
   Famous people of the War of 1812 / Robin Johnson.

(Documenting the War of 1812)
Includes bibliographical references and index.
Issued also in electronic format.
ISBN 978-0-7787-7959-9 (bound).--ISBN 978-0-7787-7964-3 (pbk.)

   1. United States--History--War of 1812--Biography--Juvenile literature. 2. Canada--History--War of 1812--Biography--Juvenile literature. I. Title. II. Series: Documenting the War of 1812

E353.J64 2011   j973.5'20922   C2011-905243-1

Library of Congress Cataloging-in-Publication Data

Johnson, Robin (Robin R.)
   Famous people of the War of 1812 / by Robin Johnson.
      p. cm. -- (Documenting the War of 1812)
   Includes bibliographical references and index.
   ISBN 978-0-7787-7959-9 (reinforced library binding : alk. paper) -- ISBN 978-0-7787-7964-3 (pbk. : alk. paper) -- ISBN 978-1-4271-8828-1 (electronic pdf) -- ISBN 978-1-4271-9731-3 (electronic html)
   1. United States--History--War of 1812--Biography--Juvenile literature. 2. United States--History--War of 1812--Sources--Juvenile literature. I. Title. II. Series.

E354.J67 2011
973.5'2--dc23
                                                                  2011029839

Crabtree Publishing Company

www.crabtreebooks.com   1-800-387-7650

Printed in the U.S.A./03013/SN20130122

**Published in Canada
Crabtree Publishing**
616 Welland Ave.
St. Catharines, Ontario
L2M 5V6

**Published in the United States
Crabtree Publishing**
PMB 59051
350 Fifth Avenue, 59th Floor
New York, New York 10118

**Published in the United Kingdom
Crabtree Publishing**
Maritime House
Basin Road North, Hove
BN41 1WR

**Published in Australia
Crabtree Publishing**
3 Charles Street
Coburg North
VIC, 3058

CONTENTS

This book includes images of, and excerpts and quotes from, documents of the War of 1812. The documents range from letters, posters, and official papers to battle plans, paintings, and cartoons.

INTRODUCTION

The War of 1812 was a historic conflict between the United States and Great Britain including its provinces in British North America, now Canada. The war lasted for more than two and a half years and left several thousands of people dead. When it was over, British North Americans (Canadians), Britons, and Americans all celebrated their victories, honored their heroes, and discovered new pride in their countries. Native North Americans mourned the loss of their last chance to preserve their ancestral lands from relentless American westward expansion.

On June 18, 1812, U.S. President James Madison declared war on Great Britain and began attacking Upper Canada. Americans were angry that the British Royal Navy

Below: A cartoon from 1813 shows King George III of Great Britain and U.S. President James Madison in a boxing match. The king has a blackened eye and bleeding nose to represent British naval losses in the war, in particular the defeat of the British warship H.M.S. *Boxer*.

was interfering with U.S. merchant ships. They also believed that Great Britain was helping Native people protect their lands, which prevented the United States from expanding to the north and west. Many Americans also wanted to capture Upper Canada (now Ontario) to make it part of the United States.

The war was fought in three theaters, or areas of conflict. In the western territories and Great Lakes, the frontier between the United States and Canada was the site of many bloody battles. Both sides struggled to control the waterways. In the Atlantic theater, men battled on ships at sea and in cities near the Atlantic coast. In the southern theater, land battles were won and lost in the Gulf Coast and swampy southern territories.

History was made in each theater of war. There were surprising victories and crushing defeats. Soldiers fought and died on the battlefields and at sea. Ordinary people did incredible things to protect or inspire their countries. This book tells some of those stories.

Left: Many Americans believed that the United States would easily win the War of 1812 since Great Britain was preoccupied with a war with France. After the first few battles, this notion quickly evaporated. (Shawnee chief Tecumseh is pictured here shaking hands with British Major-General Isaac Brock.)

Theaters of war—where the battles took place

When the United States declared war on Great Britain in 1812, the republic consisted of 18 states and a number of territories that had yet to be organized and admitted to the Union. British North America (now Canada) was divided into several provinces that included Upper Canada (Ontario) and Lower Canada (Quebec). In the north, U.S. troops invaded Canada and were in turn attacked by British forces and Native allies from Canada. Naval actions took place on the Great Lakes and Lake Champlain. In the east, British ships blockaded U.S. ports and British troops attacked Washington, D.C., and Baltimore. In the south, fighting occurred in Mississippi, Florida, and Louisiana.

Right: A map of the war shows the locations of major battles.

Below: A map of North America shows country, state, and territory boundaries as they were in 1812.

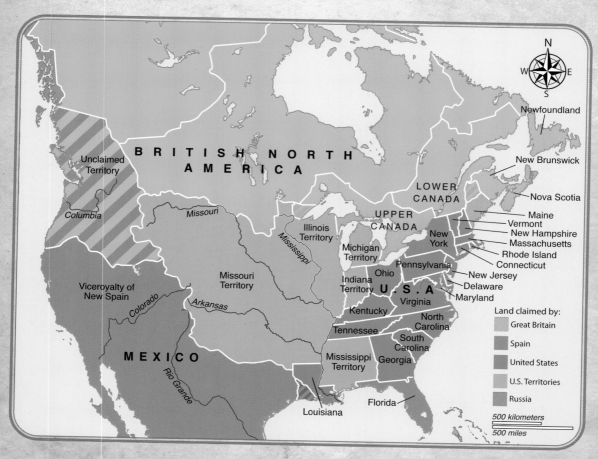

BRITISH NORTH AMERICA

Unclaimed Territory

Columbia

Missouri

LOWER CANADA

UPPER CANADA

Illinois Territory

Michigan Territory

Newfoundland

New Brunswick

Nova Scotia

Maine
Vermont
New Hampshire
Massachusetts
Rhode Island
Connecticut

New York

Pennsylvania

Ohio

Indiana Territory

U . S . A

New Jersey

Delaware

Maryland

Missouri Territory

Viceroyalty of New Spain

Colorado

Arkansas

Kentucky

Tennessee

Virginia

North Carolina

South Carolina

MEXICO

Mississippi

Rio Grande

Mississippi Territory

Georgia

Louisiana

Florida

Land claimed by:

Great Britain

Spain

United States

U.S. Territories

Russia

500 kilometers

500 miles

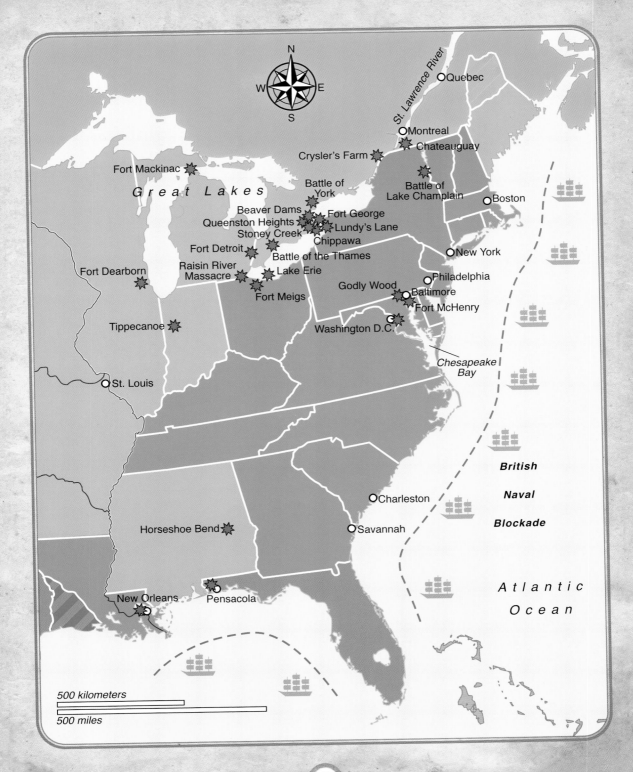

Quebec

St. Lawrence River

Montreal

Chateauguay

Crysler's Farm

Fort Mackinac

Battle of
Lake Champlain

Boston

G r e a t   L a k e s

Battle of
York

Beaver Dams

Fort George

Queenston Heights

Lundy's Lane

Stoney Creek

Chippawa

Fort Detroit

Battle of the Thames

New York

Fort Dearborn

Raisin River
Massacre

Lake Erie

Philadelphia

Godly Wood

Baltimore

Fort Meigs

Fort McHenry

Tippecanoe

Washington D.C.

*Chesapeake
Bay*

St. Louis

Charleston

British

Naval

Horseshoe Bend

Savannah

Blockade

A t l a n t i c

New Orleans

Pensacola

O c e a n

500 kilometers

500 miles

Chapter One: People in the Lead-up to the War

Below: British-born American sailors were taken from their U.S. ships and forced to fight for the British Royal Navy.

Starting in the early 1800s, Great Britain and France began blocking merchant ships from reaching each other's shores to cut off their supplies. U.S. merchant ships were blocked, and U.S. trade suffered. Then, to maintain its large navy, the British impressed, or forced, men into serving in their navy. They considered British-born Americans to be eligible. British ships began to stop U.S. merchant ships and force U.S. sailors to join the British Royal Navy.

The United States was growing fast. In 1809, the country bought huge areas of land from Native North Americans. Some Native people tried to stop Americans from settling them. The British further irritated the Americans by giving agricultural tools, household goods, and guns and ammunition to the Native people. Many of the guns were used to attack white settlers and defend Native land.

In His Own Words

A Loyalist named Mather Byles wondered if it was better *"to be ruled by one tyrant three thousand miles away, or by three thousand tyrants not a mile away."*

Loyalists versus Patriots

United Empire Loyalists were Americans who stayed true to Britain during the American Revolutionary War. When that war ended in 1783, about 50,000 Loyalists left the United States and many settled in Canada. Thousands left because they disagreed with the Republican views of many Americans (see page 12). As well, many Americans left the United States to settle in Upper Canada where land was free.

By 1812 most of the inhabitants of Upper Canada were American-born and many came from families who had fought against the British in the American Revolution. Nevertheless, during the War of 1812 they fought against their former American neighbors to defend their new homes in Canada.

Below: Many Loyalists were forced out of their homes by angry Patriots, who were colonists that had fought against Britain.

William Henry Harrison

As Governor of Indiana Territory from 1801, William Henry Harrison tried to obtain lands from Native North Americans to expand and increase American settlements and population. A treaty of 1804 led to Harrison obtaining much of western Illinois and parts of Missouri from the Sauk, who were angered by the event.

Harrison was involved in a more serious conflict with Native people in 1811. Shawnee chief Tecumseh had tried to set up a confederation of Native North Americans to fight again the U.S. land grabs. Americans believed that the Shawnee were being helped by the British. On November 7, 1811, at the Battle of Tippecanoe, U.S. forces led by Harrison destroyed Tecumseh's village. This ill feeling toward the British influenced the U.S. government to declare war on Great Britain only six months later.

Below: This broadside from Harrison's 1840 presidential election campaign depicts some of his exploits during the War of 1812. Harrison won the election but held office for only one month, before dying on April 4, 1841, of pneumonia.

Above: This portrait of William Henry Harrison was painted in 1840, the year he was elected ninth U.S. president.

Tecumseh

In 1811, a brilliant comet blazed across the sky. Tecumseh, a Shawnee war chief whose name meant "shooting star," claimed it was a sign of his power. Many agreed. U.S. Governor William Henry Harrison called him "one of those uncommon geniuses."

Tecumseh believed that Native people needed to work together to protect their territory from the expanding United States. He traveled to many Native nations and urged them to form a confederacy. Tecumseh also felt that the land belonged to all the nations who shared it. Therefore, it could not be sold by any one nation. He cried, "Sell a country! Why not sell the air, the clouds, and the great sea, as well as the earth?"

Below: This portrait of Shawnee chief Tecumseh was painted after his death.

Right: Tecumseh (depicted on the right, falling to the ground) was a skilled warrior and a valuable ally to the British Army. He was killed in the war by a U.S. soldier on October 5, 1813, during the Battle of the Thames.

Although he was unable to form a lasting confederacy, Tecumseh had many followers from other Native nations. Together, they joined forces with the British and fought the United States in the War of 1812.

Thomas Jefferson

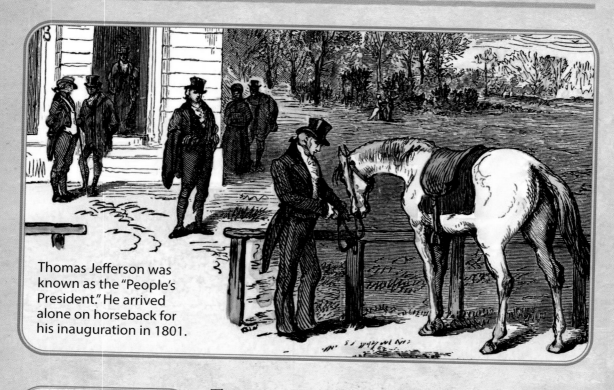

Thomas Jefferson was known as the "People's President." He arrived alone on horseback for his inauguration in 1801.

Being a Republican

Like many Americans of the time, Jefferson had strong Republican views. A Republican government is one ruled by its citizens rather than by a hereditary monarch—like Britain's king or queen. Citizens elect their leaders, who must follow the country's laws.

Thomas Jefferson is regarded as one of the greatest leaders in the history of the United States. He was president from 1801 to 1809. During that time, Jefferson made many decisions that shaped the country. In 1803, he bought an enormous area of land in North America from France. The deal was known as the Louisiana Purchase. It doubled the size of the United States. Jefferson later sent a group of men led by Meriwether Lewis and William Clark to explore and map the land so it could be settled.

At the same time the United States was expanding, its ships were going nowhere. In 1807, Jefferson ordered an embargo that prevented U.S. merchant ships from sailing to foreign countries. Jefferson's intention was to make Britain and France end their own trade blockades, thus avoiding war. Ironically, the embargo hurt the United States the most, and helped steer the country toward war instead of away from it.

Sir George Prevost

Hard Times in New England

New England relied heavily on shipping. With Jefferson's embargo in place, ships were forced to drop anchor indefinitely. People struggled to put food on the table. Not surprisingly, most New Englanders spoke out loudly against the war.

Below: In the 1770s, an artist painted this view in Lower Canada (Quebec), making it look like a European city of the time.

Sir George Prevost was a strong but cautious leader. As Commander-in-Chief and Governor-General of British North America (Canada) during the War of 1812, his small army defended against many attacks. Under his direction, officers such as Major-General Isaac Brock strengthened the British North American forces and held off the greater number of U.S. troops with few weapons and men.

Prevost's contributions before the war were equally important. His senior officers prepared British North American citizens and forts to survive a U.S. attack. Prevost also encouraged New Englanders to ignore U.S. President Thomas Jefferson's embargo against trading with France, and Britain and its provinces. He created "free ports" where duties, or taxes, were not charged on goods. By doing so, Prevost was able to get war supplies from the very country he would soon be fighting.

James Madison

James Madison is often called the "Father of the Constitution." As the fourth president of the United States, he led his country from 1809 to 1817. Madison's decision to lead his country to war with Britain in 1812, however, was not a popular one.

Madison was encouraged to fight by the War Hawks. The War Hawks were vocal members of the U.S. Congress who wanted to wage war on Great Britain. They were eager to invade Canada and felt that it would be easy to do so.

Although the United States was not prepared for a large-scale war, Madison declared war on June 18, 1812. It was the first time the United States had ever declared war on another country.

Below: This portrait shows James Madison during his presidency.

Left: When President Madison signed this Official Declaration of War, the United States entered into war with Great Britain.

In Senate of the U. States

June 17th 1812.

The Confidential bill from the House of Representatives, entitled "An act declaring war between Great Britain and her dependencies, and the United States, and their territories," was read the third time.

Whereupon, Resolved, That the said bill do pass with the following amendments.

Line 3. Strike out the words "Great Britain and her dependencies," and insert "the United Kingdom of Great Britain and Ireland and the dependencies thereof."

Line 4. After the word "states" where it first occurs, insert "of America."

Line — the words "Government of" strike out to the end of the ... ...ited Kingdom of Great Britain

Chapter Two: In the Western Territories and Great Lakes

Thomas Jefferson said that acquiring Canada would be a "mere matter of marching." This would be disproved by British Major-General Brock's leadership of a small but well-trained group of British forces assisted by British North Americans and Native allies.

Left: U.S. volunteers in the War of 1812 gather in the streets of Philadelphia, ready to do battle.

The Militia

When the War of 1812 began, neither side was ready for battle. Most British forces were fighting in Europe, leaving some 6,000 soldiers to defend Upper and Lower Canada. The United States had about three times as many soldiers. Both countries also had militia.

A militia is a fighting force made up of ordinary citizens that supports a regular army during times of conflict. During the War of 1812, the American militia was poorly trained. Most men had never fought before and had few supplies. Nevertheless, the militia did much of the fighting for both countries, especially in the western territories and Great Lakes theater.

Sir Isaac Brock

Sir Isaac Brock was called "The Hero of Upper Canada." He was a bold leader and a brilliant strategist. As Major-General and commander-in-chief of regular and militia forces in Upper Canada, Brock enthusiastically commanded his troops.

Before the war, Brock strengthened forts and forces in Upper Canada. He recruited volunteers into the militia and made sure they were properly trained. He also strengthened alliances with First Nations from Upper Canada and Native Americans.

Below: This modern statue honors the war hero Major-General Brock. When Canadians were prepared to surrender, Brock wrote: "Most of the people have lost all confidence—I however speak loud and look big."

BROCK

Pushing on

Brock led his men to two important victories early in the war. At the Siege of Detroit, his forces were outnumbered two to one. Brock attacked Fort Detroit anyway. He dressed his civilian militia in old red army coats to make it appear as if his regular red-uniformed British force of well trained men was greater than it actually was. U.S. General William Hull, who at nearly 60 years old had been reluctant to take on command again, surrendered Detroit and all of Michigan.

Brock's unlikely victory made him an instant hero. It also gave Canadians the determination to fight on. Brock was killed in the Battle of Queenston Heights on October 13, 1812.

John Brant

John Brant, known also by his Mohawk name Ahyonwaeghs, was a young Mohawk war chief and a royal ally of the British. He was the son of Joseph Brant, a famous Mohawk military and political leader allied with the British during the American Revolution. John assisted the main Mohawk war chief, John Norton, in encouraging the Six Nations of the Grand River to defend their lands. During the War of 1812, Brant and Norton fought alongside the militia of Upper Canada and British troops in key battles.

On October 13, 1812, U.S. forces attacked Queenston Heights. General Brock was killed early in the battle. That afternoon Brant and Norton with 80 Mohawk warriors joined the final British charge that ended the battle. British General Roger Hale Sheaffe, who had been born in Boston before the American Revolution, defeated the invading U.S. army in the first major battle of the War of 1812.

In His Own Words

A Canadian militia officer described the actions of Brant and his men that day:

"The Indians were the first in advance. As soon as they perceived the enemy they uttered their terrific war-whoop, and commenced a most destructive fire, rushing rapidly upon them. Our troops instantly sprang forward from all quarters, joining in the shout. The Americans stood a few moments ... and then fled by hundreds down the mountain."

Above: This portrait shows Mohawk chief John Brant.

Left: John Brant's father, Joseph Brant, was a well-known Mohawk leader.

Laura Secord

Below: Legend has it that Secord brought a cow with her to hide the real reason for her journey. The story is untrue and was invented by a playwright in the mid-1800s to add drama to the story.

Laura Ingersoll Secord was an ordinary woman with extraordinary courage. Born in Massachussets, she moved with her Loyalist family to Queenston in Upper Canada after the American Revolution.

On June 21, 1813, Secord was said to have overheard U.S. soldiers planning a surprise attack on the British outpost of Beaver Dams. Her husband had been injured in the Battle of Queenston Heights and was unable to travel. So Secord set out early the next morning to warn the British herself. She walked about 20 miles (32 kilometers) through thick woods and wide streams.

After an 18-hour trek, Secord was finally able to deliver her message to British Lieutenant James Fitzgibbon. Two days later, Native allies ambushed the U.S. soldiers. The Battle of Beaver Dams ended with the surrender of some 500 Americans to the British. Long after her death, Secord became a celebrated Canadian heroine.

Fanny Doyle

Women were sometimes allowed to accompany their husbands in war campaigns, and did during the War of 1812. They often did jobs such as laundry, cooking, nursing, and serving. Fanny Doyle, sometimes called Betsy Doyle, was the wife of an American artillery private. She accompanied her husband into military service during the War of 1812. Her husband was captured in the Battle of Queenston Heights. Fanny Doyle showed the men she could do more than the laundry when she fought with "extraordinary bravery" on November 12, 1812, during a heavy artillery fight between the American-held Fort Niagara and the British-held Fort George. During the fighting Fanny operated a small cannon on the mess-roof at Fort Niagara. Her efforts were later praised by American Lieutenant Colonel George Mcfeeley.

Left: An engraving shows Fanny Doyle operating a cannon at Fort Niagara.

Below: Today, Fort Niagara is a National Historic Landmark and popular tourist attraction.

Robert Heriot Barclay

Robert Heriot Barclay was a British naval officer who led a small squadron of ships that enabled the British to move supplies on Lake Erie. Despite some initial success, Barclay eventually had to withdraw. Most of his sailors were poorly trained and the squadron had few supplies or weapons such as long-range cannons. U.S. Commodore Oliver Hazard Perry took control of the lake. Barclay wrote to his commanding officer:

...It is the opinion of the Major General Commanding the forces here that some thing must be attempted by me to enable us to get Supplies by the Lake...

That such a thing is necessary, there cannot be a doubt... I shall sail and risk every thing to gain so great a point, as that of opening the communication by water.

That the Risk is very great I feel very much...

R.H. Barclay

Despite the danger, Barclay had no choice but to lead his men into the Battle of Lake Erie on September 10, 1813. Many British were killed or wounded. The Americans took possession of their ships and the lake.

Below: An 1814 drawing by artist Thomas Birch shows the U.S. fleet under command of Perry engaged in battle with Barclay's forces on Lake Erie.

Oliver Hazard Perry

Oliver Hazard Perry wrote an entirely different letter to his commanding officer. Perry was the celebrated U.S. naval captain who defeated Barclay on Lake Erie. When the British surrendered, Perry sent this battle report to his commanding officer: "We have met the enemy and they are ours: two ships, two brigs, one schooner and one sloop."

Although Perry's message was famously short, his actions at the Battle of Lake Erie spoke for themselves. Perry's flagship, the U.S.S. *Lawrence*, came under heavy attack and was almost destroyed. He did not stop fighting, however. Instead, Perry rowed through heavy gunfire to reach another ship in his fleet. From there, he continued to command U.S. forces until they won the battle. It was the first major victory for the United States in the War of 1812.

Above: Perry's ships fire cannons at the British ships.

Left: Captain Perry wrote this short note that sent a very encouraging message to his commander.

> We have met the enemy and they are ours:
> Two Ships, two Brigs one Schooner & one Sloop.
> Yours, with great respect and esteem
> O H Perry.

Charles de Salaberry

Charles-Michel d'Irumberry de Salaberry was a French-Canadian born in Beauport, Lower Canada, in 1778. De Salaberry volunteered for military service when he was just 14 years old and was a veteran officer of the British army. In 1812, Lieutenant Colonel de Salaberry was put in charge of recruiting and training a French-Canadian militia unit called the Voltigeurs. They became one of Canada's best fighting units.

In September 1813, de Salaberry got news that the Americans were planning to attack Montreal to cut off supply lines to the British in Upper Canada. In the Battle of Chateauguay, de Salaberry set up camp in the Chateauguay Valley, where the American soldiers would come through. The American forces led by General Wade Hampton outnumbered de Salaberry's forces. Even so, de Salaberry was able to hold the American forces back by destroying the pathway through the valley, and tricking them into thinking there were more British forces than what there really were. Hampton led an attack on October 26, but was stopped by the British and retreated. Charles de Salaberry's Voltigeurs also fought at the Battle of Crysler's Farm. The British, the Voltigeurs, and Mohawk warriors were outnumbered by even more American forces. Charles de Salaberry's clever fighting strategies brought the British yet another victory on that day, too.

Above: A statue of Charles de Salaberry stands at the Parliament Building in Quebec, Canada.

Red George Macdonell

George Richard John Macdonell, known as Red George because of his red hair, was born in St. John's, Newfoundland, in 1780. He recruited the Glengarry Light Infantry Fencibles in 1811, and became lieutenant colonel for the force and took over command of Fort Wellington at Prescott, in Upper Canada.

Macdonell led the Glengarry Light Infantry and attacked the American forces at Ogdensburg, New York, on February 22, 1813. His action helped to secure the St. Lawrence River between Upper and Lower Canada. He later took command of the 1st Light Infantry Battalion at Kingston and joined Charles-Michel de Salaberry at the Battle of Chateauguay in October of 1813. At the end of the war he helped plan an alternative canal route along the Rideau River and lakes.

Below: A scene from the Battle of Chateauguay shows Canadian troops led by Charles de Salaberry defeating the invading American army.

Sir Gordon Drummond

Lieutenant-General Gordon Drummond was the first officer born in what is now Canada to command a British Army in Upper Canada.

Drummond took command of the forces in Canada at the end of 1813. Within two weeks he ordered his troops to make an assault on Fort Niagara after the British had retaken Fort George. The successful attack raised the spirits of the British troops and the militia in Upper Canada. More successful attacks followed.

Then, on July 25, 1814, Drummond led his men at the Battle of Lundy's Lane. It was one of the bloodiest battles ever fought in Canada, with more than 850 casualties on each side. The Americans retreated to Fort Erie. Drummond followed them and started a two-month siege. When he thought all was ready he attacked but was beaten back with heavy casualites. Drummond finally gave up the siege on September 15, and marched his men back to Fort George.

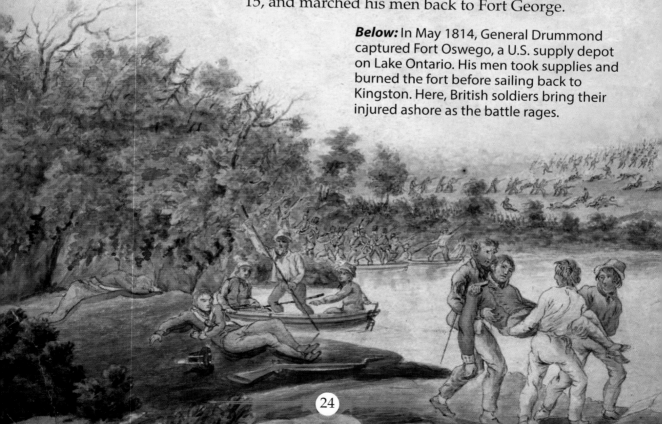

Below: In May 1814, General Drummond captured Fort Oswego, a U.S. supply depot on Lake Ontario. His men took supplies and burned the fort before sailing back to Kingston. Here, British soldiers bring their injured ashore as the battle rages.

Jacob Jennings Brown

Below: A portrait shows Jacob Brown in his military uniform.

Pennsylvania-born Jacob Jennings Brown began his military career fighting in the militia. In May of 1813, his forces successfully defended Sackett's Harbor, the main U.S. shipyard on Lake Ontario. The important victory earned him a high rank in the regular army. In July of 1814, General Brown's troops easily captured Fort Erie. His army of 4,500 overwhelmed the 137 British soldiers defending the fort. Brown then advanced toward Niagara fighting the Battle of Chippawa on July 5. His army of 3,500 men beat a British force of 2,100. This was the first time that an American army had beaten a regular-army enemy of roughly equal size on an open battlefield.

Brown's attack on Lundy's Lane, however, was not successful. After many hours of bloody combat, no ground was captured. Forces on both sides suffered horrendous losses, and the Americans retreated to Fort Erie. Brown's men outlasted a siege of the fort, but in the end, they abandoned and destroyed it themselves.

James Miller

At Lundy's Lane, Brown ordered Colonel James Miller to capture the British artillery. Miller launched a bold attack, getting the guns and driving back the enemy. Although the guns were retaken by the British the next day, Miller had earned himself the name "Hero of Lundy's Lane."

Winfield Scott

Born in Petersburg, Virginia, Winfield Scott joined the U.S. Army in 1808 and took part in three wars: the War of 1812, the Mexican-American War, and the American Civil War. During the War of 1812, he climbed in rank to major general.

In the War of 1812, Colonel Scott led attacks against British, Canadian, and Native forces in Upper Canada between Fort George and Fort Erie. British forces captured Scott and over 900 of his men when they surrendered on October 13, 1812, at the Battle of Queenston Heights. He regained his freedom in a prisoner exchange and went on to lead the capture of Fort George in May 1813.

In the spring of 1814, Scott trained an American brigade in Buffalo, New York. Known as "Old Fuss and Feathers" for his insistence on military discipline, Scott is credited with turning his band of regulars and volunteers into well trained soldiers that were the equal of British regulars. In July of 1814, he distinguished himself at both the Battle of Chippawa and the Battle of Lundy's Lane. He lost many men at Lundy's Lane and he himself was wounded.

Above: American general, Winfield Scott is shown in this photograph taken in 1861.

Below: A colored engraving shows Winfield Scott and his American troops at the Battle of Chippawa.

Thomas Macdonough

Thomas Macdonough led the United States to a celebrated victory on Lake Champlain, defeating one British attack and forcing another to be abandoned.

On September 11, 1814, Britain's land and naval forces planned a two-pronged attack to capture Plattsburgh in New York State. A British flotilla began the assault by attacking U.S. vessels in Plattsburgh Bay. Macdonough's flagship, the U.S.S. *Saratoga*, was hit hard in the intense, close-range, two-hour battle, which took out all the guns on one side of the vessel.

Macdonough used the *Saratoga*'s anchors to swing the ship around. He then attacked using the guns from the undamaged side of the ship. The three main British vessels surrendered and the British gunboats retreated. Without the support of its navy, the British attack by land was cancelled. Macdonough would be forever remembered as the "Hero of Lake Champlain."

In His Own Words

"In this situation, the whole force, on both sides, became engaged, the Saratoga suffering much from the heavy fire … Our guns on the starboard side being nearly all dismounted or not manageable, a stern anchor was let go … and the ship winded, with a fresh broadside on the enemy's ship, which soon after surrendered."
—Captain Macdonough

Right: A contemporary portrait of Thomas Macdonough shows him in his naval uniform.

Chapter Three: Great and Good of the Atlantic Theater

When the War of 1812 began, the British Royal Navy had around 600 ships. It was the world's largest naval force. However, many British ships were already being used in the Napoleonic Wars leaving only a very small number available for the defense of British North America.

The Americans had only 17 warships that were seaworthy. The ships were big and sturdy, however. One ship, the U.S.S. *Constitution*, was nicknamed "Old Ironsides." U.S. sailors claimed their shots bounced off the wooden ship as though it were made of iron.

Battles in the Atlantic theater were mostly single-ship actions. Some conflicts took place in the middle of the ocean, while others were fought in areas closer to shore. Fighting in the Atlantic theater also moved onto land, where British troops boldly attacked Washington, Baltimore, and a number of other coastal locations.

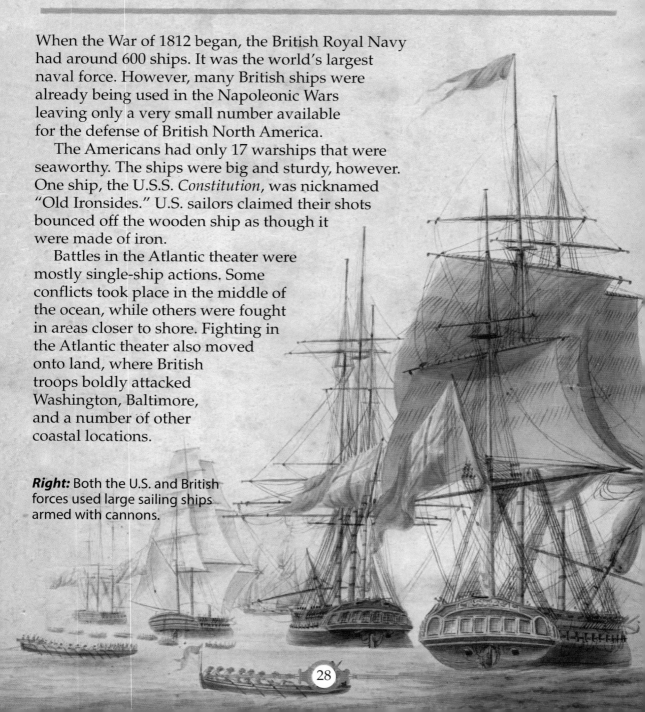

Right: Both the U.S. and British forces used large sailing ships armed with cannons.

Isaac Hull

Isaac Hull was an American naval Captain and Commodore who fought on the Atlantic Ocean. He was the nephew of General William Hull (see page 16), but he enjoyed more success than his uncle in the War of 1812.

Isaac Hull captained the U.S.S. *Constitution*. The *Constitution* was a sturdy frigate, or warship. On August 19, 1812, Hull met a smaller British frigate called the H.M.S. *Guerriere* off the coast of Nova Scotia. The *Constitution* had more and larger cannons, and many more crew than the *Guerriere*. Hull waited until the attacking ship was very close. Then he shouted to his crew, "Now, boys, pour it into them!" His guns hit their mark and the British soon surrendered. Hull burned the remains of the *Guerriere* and sailed home a hero.

Hull's victory raised the morale of his entire country. His triumph proved that the United States could take on the powerful Royal Navy—and come out sailing.

Above: Captain Isaac Hull

Below: British frigate H.M.S. *Guerriere* is captured by the U.S.S. *Constitution*.

Stephen Decatur

Above: Captain Decatur

Below: The U.S.S. *United States* (right) commanded by Decatur overcomes the British ship H.M.S. *Macedonian*.

Stephen Decatur was the youngest captain in the history of the U.S. Navy. His heroism in earlier wars earned Decatur the high rank at the age of 25.

In the War of 1812, Decatur commanded a large 44-gun frigate called the U.S.S. *United States*. On the morning of October 25, 1812, Decatur spied an enemy ship off the Canary Islands. He launched an aggressive attack on the ship, a British frigate called the H.M.S. *Macedonian*. The *Macedonian* was half the size of the *United States*. By noon, Decatur had destroyed the ship's masts and captured its crew.

Decatur repaired the *Macedonian* and sailed home with it. It was the first captured British ship that was brought back to the United States. Americans celebrated and sang:

"Then quickly met our nation's eyes
The noblest sight in nature—
A first-rate frigate as a prize
Brought home by brave Decatur."

Sir George Cockburn

Sir George Cockburn was a British naval commander who was feared by many. Stationed at Chesapeake Bay during the War of 1812, he launched a "campaign of terror" on U.S. citizens, intent on forcing the Americans to negotiate a quick end to the war. He raided, plundered, and burned many homes and farms around the bay in retaliation for the destruction by the Americans of the town of Niagara and the village of St. David's in Upper Canada.

Cockburn then provided the transport for British Major-General Ross to attack Washington. On August 24, 1814, the British burned the Capitol, the White House, and other buildings in retaliation for the destruction of public buildings by the Americans at York, the captial of Upper Canada. In Washington, many priceless items—and the morale of the American people—were destroyed in the blaze.

Above: Rear Admiral Cockburn led Britain's charge on Washington.

Below: The empty shell of the White House—the U.S. president's home—after the burning of Washington, D.C.

In His Own Words

"*The Enemy opened upon us a heavy fire of Musquetry from the Capitol and two other houses, these were therefore almost immediately Stormed by our People, taken possession of, and set on fire, after which the Town submitted without further resistance … We also set fire to the Presidents Palace, the Treasury, and the War Office, and in the morning… destroyed whatever Stores and Buildings had escaped the Flames …*"
—Rear Admiral George Cockburn

Sir Philip Broke

Sir Philip Broke achieved Britain's first major naval victory in the War of 1812. Broke's victory restored confidence within the Royal Navy. To that point they had lost in ship-to-ship actions against more powerful U.S. frigates.

Broke took command of the H.M.S. *Shannon* in 1806. He was a gunnery expert who spent the next seven years preparing the 38-gun frigate and training his crew. When he met the U.S.S. *Chesapeake* off Boston Harbor, Broke was ready for battle.

On June 1, 1813, the Americans attacked. Within minutes, Captain Broke and his skilled crew had gunned down many of the *Chesapeake*'s men and destroyed the ship's wheel. The British boarded and captured the ship. The entire battle lasted only 11 minutes but left nearly 150 Americans killed or wounded. The *Shannon* showed what could be done against a U.S. ship that was equal in size.

James Lawrence

James Lawrence commanded the U.S.S. *Chesapeake*. Although he lost the ship to Broke, he became a legendary figure of the war with his dying words.

Captain Lawrence took command of the *Chesapeake* on May 20, 1813. Less than two weeks later, he launched a bold single-ship attack on the H.M.S. *Shannon*. Lawrence was encouraged by the earlier triumphs of his fellow officers at sea. He was not prepared for Broke's expertly trained crew and their fierce attack on his ship.

Lawrence was mortally wounded early in the battle, but he refused to surrender the *Chesapeake*. As he was being carried below deck, he cried, "Tell the men to fire faster! Don't give up the ship!" The fight was lost and his men did give up the ship as soon as Lawrence was out of sight. But his dying command became a battle cry for the U.S. Navy.

Below: The U.S.S. *Chesapeake* (left) approaches the H.M.S. *Shannon* in this painting by artist Robert Dodd in 1813.

DONT GIVE UP THE SHIP

Above: Captain Lawrence's famous words encouraged Americans to fight. Lawrence's friend, Captain Perry, flew this flag at the Battle of Lake Erie.

Robert Ross

Robert Ross was a respected British army officer, admired for both his courage and his compassion. He led his troops to historic victories at Bladensburg and Washington during the War of 1812.

On his way to attack Washington, D.C., Ross and his forces met up against U.S. troops at Bladensburg. The Americans fought with almost 7,000 men and 18 cannons against the British force with 4,500 men, three cannons, and 60 rocket launchers. U.S. regulars and sailors stood their ground for a brief period but the militia ran off in panic. The defeat allowed the British to continue to Washington. As Ross approached the city, his horse was shot out from under him. Important public buildings were burned, but Ross was said to have ordered that private property be spared.

Left: A cartoon of the time shows the American militia (left) repelling British soldiers in Baltimore.

Below: Major-General Ross was killed during the Battle of North Point.

Ross's next target was the busy port city of Baltimore. On September 12, 1814, Ross and his troops landed outside the city at North Point. The U.S. militia was expecting them. Ross rode forward to command his troops and was killed by a hidden sniper. The British continued to fight and soon defeated the Americans at the Battle of North Point.

Dolley Madison

Below: This photograph from 1848 shows Dolley Madison, who was almost captured by the British while she rescued national treasures from the White House.

Dolley Payne Todd Madison was the First Lady of the United States—the president's wife—during the War of 1812. She was a lively and jolly hostess who entertained society with her warmth and charm. She was also a brave and patriotic heroine who risked her life to save national treasures.

While the British prepared to burn Washington, Madison rescued priceless items—including her husband's letters and a large portrait of George Washington—from the White House. She also took time to write to her sister:

"We have had a battle or skirmish near Bladensburg, and I am still here within sound of the cannon! Mr. Madison comes not; may God protect him! Two messengers covered with dust, come to bid me fly; but I wait for him. . . . At this late hour a wagon has been procured, I have had it filled with the plate and most valuable portable articles belonging to the house . . ."

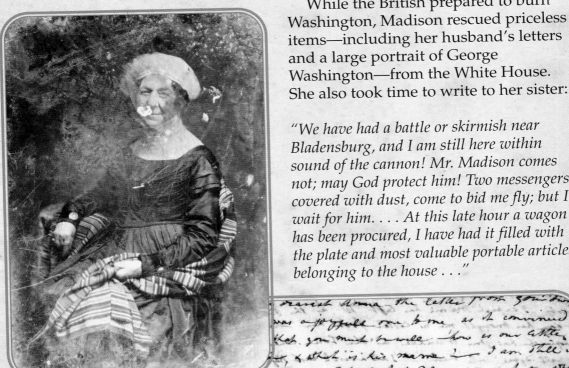

Right: Part of another letter from Dolley Madison to her sister, Anna Cutts, describes life as the president's wife.

Sir Alexander Cochrane

While Ross led Great Britain's land attack on Baltimore, Sir Alexander Cochrane attacked by sea. Cochrane was an aggressive and experienced commander who was determined to take Fort McHenry.

Early on September 13, 1814, Cochrane and his fleet of 19 ships began attacking. They bombarded the fort with rockets, bombs, and cannonballs for nearly 25 hours. The Americans, however, had sunk a line of ships in the mouth of the harbor so the British could not get within effective range. The bombardment did little damage, and the Americans refused to surrender.

The next morning, Cochrane pulled out his ships and set sail for New Orleans. He planned to keep attacking the Americans until they were "drubbed into good manners."

Inset: This letter from U.S. President Madison to the privateer ship *Abaellino* gave it permission to attack and capture British ships.

Below: Fort McHenry in Baltimore, Maryland, as it is today. The fort is an official national monument and historic shrine.

The Pride of Baltimore

Cochrane targeted Baltimore because many U.S. privateer ships were built there. One of the most successful privateers to set sail from the harbor was Captain Thomas Boyle. He captured 17 British merchant ships during the War of 1812. Boyle and his ship, the *Chasseur*, became the "Pride of Baltimore."

George Armistead

Inset: Armistead commissioned Mary Pickersgill to create an enormous flag for the fort. It measured 30 by 42 feet (9 x 13 meters). The flag had more than one million stitches, all sewn by hand.

George Armistead was the commander of Fort McHenry. He defended the star-shaped fort against the British forces—and became a star himself.

Before the Battle of Baltimore, Major Armistead strengthened Fort McHenry and readied his soldiers for war. When the British attacked, Armistead's troops returned fire. Their guns could not reach the British ships, however. The Americans were helpless. As one soldier put it, "We were like pigeons tied by the legs to be shot at." However, the British fleet were too far out and could not fire effectively on the fort.

Although the Americans were bombarded for a full day and night, Armistead refused to give up Fort McHenry. Instead, on September 14, 1814, he raised the U.S. flag over the fort, a symbol to the British that Armistead would not surrender. The British realized that their bombardment was having few results, so they abandoned the attack and sailed away.

Francis Scott Key

On September 14, 1814, Francis Scott Key saw Mary Pickersgill's flag flying over Fort McHenry. It inspired him to write some very famous poems.

Key was an American lawyer who was held on a British ship during the Battle of Baltimore. He watched "the bombs bursting in air" as the British attacked the fort throughout the night. The next morning, "by the dawn's early light," he saw the "broad stripes and bright stars" of the U.S. flag still waving in the distance over Fort McHenry. The big flag sent Key a big message: The United States had not surrendered.

Key wrote a patriotic poem called "The Defense of Fort McHenry." The poem—set to music and renamed "The Star-Spangled Banner"—later became the national anthem of the United States of America.

Below: Although used as the national song since the 1880s, "The Star Spangled Banner" was made the official national anthem by Congress in 1931.

Above: Francis Scott Key

Chapter Four: The Fight in the Southern Theater

On December 24, 1814, representatives of Great Britain and the United States signed a peace treaty. The Treaty of Ghent ended the War of 1812. Signed in Belgium, news of the treaty did not reach the United States for some time as it had to be delivered across the Atlantic by ship. In the meantime, the countries continued to fight in the Southern theater.

The British were determined to force the Americans to respect treaties they had made with the Native people and land rights west of the Mississippi. The Americans, however, considered it their right to continue to push westward on to Native lands without interference. They fought hard to protect their territory from British forces. There were few battles in the South, but they were brutal.

Below: The Battle of New Orleans was a deadly battle that took place in the Southern theater. It was fought after a peace treaty had already been signed to end the war. This painting was made by an engineer in the Louisiana Army based on a drawing he did on the battlefield.

William "Red Eagle" Weatherford

William "Red Eagle" Weatherford was a Creek warrior who led the "Red Sticks" against the Americans at the Battle of Horseshoe Bend.

The Red Sticks were members of the Creek Nation who wished to preserve a traditional way of life and protect their homeland. They fought other Creeks who felt that resisting the Americans was hopeless. The Red Sticks attacked Fort Mims in Alabama on August 30, 1813, and killed more than 500 American settlers, militia, and Creek warriors.

On March 27, 1814, Major-General Andrew Jackson led an attack on the Red Stick camp. His army had more than 3,000 men including 600 Native American allies. The Red Sticks had about 1,000 men. The Battle of Horseshoe Bend lasted just five hours. More than 850 of the 1,000 Red Sticks were killed. Weatherford surrendered. Jackson admired Weatherford's courage and spared his life.

Below: Major-General Andrew Jackson (left) takes the surrender of Chief William Weatherford after the defeat of the Red Stick Creeks at the Battle of Horseshoe Bend, Alabama.

Andrew Jackson

Andrew Jackson was an aggressive American commander. He was called "Old Hickory" because on the campaign he was as tough as hickory wood. Major-General Jackson was also called a war hero and, later, president of the United States.

After crushing the "Red Stick" Creeks, Jackson fought the British at the Battle of New Orleans. Britain had attacked the busy port on January 8, 1815. Although the British had a larger and more experienced army, it was no match for Jackson's men. Protected by strong earthworks built before the battle, the Americans used well-placed cannons, rifles, and muskets to kill row after row of approaching British soldiers. The British retreated and Jackson was celebrated as "the ablest general the United States produced."

Right: Andrew Jackson (center) commands his men during the Battle of New Orleans.

Jackson's Army

Major-General Jackson put together a large and diverse army to stop the British. His troops were made up of trained regulars, militia, and untrained fighters. There were slaves, freed slaves, rugged frontiersmen, Choctaw warriors, and even a band of pirates.

GLOSSARY

ally A group or person who joins another to achieve a common goal

ambush To make a surprise attack from a hidden position

army A large group of people trained to fight on land

artillery Large guns, such as cannons, used in war

barge A long, flat-bottomed boat used to carry cargo on rivers

bombard To attack continually using bombs, shells, or other missiles

border Dividing line between two countries, for example between Canada and the United States

campaign A series of planned military actions intended to achieve a certain goal

cannonade A period of time with continual and heavy gunfire

casualty A person who is killed or wounded in battle

civilians People not directly involved in the military or a war

colony A place where people live far from the country that rules it. The original thirteen U.S. states were once British colonies

confederacy A group of people who come together for a specific purpose

Congress In the United States, two groups of representatives who make laws for the nation. The groups are the Senate and the House of Representatives.

Constitution The set of rules that the U.S. government follows

depot A place where large amounts of goods are stored

diverse To be different from one another

document An official or original paper, such as a letter, page of a newspaper, or treaty, but also items that serve as proof or evidence, for example a photograph, painting, engraving, or poster

drub To hit or beat someone over and over again

duty A fee that must be paid when certain items are shipped into or out of a country

earthworks A large bank of soil made as a defense

embargo An order to stop trading with another country for a certain period of time

excerpt A small part of a letter, book, or other written document

flagship The ship that carries the commander of a fleet

fleet A group of ships in a country's navy

flotilla A small fleet of ships

Founding Father One of several leaders who fought for American independence and helped create the United States

free trade Trade between nations without interference, such as tariffs or taxes, from government

frigate A mid-size warship used during the 1800s

frontier A line or border that separates two countries

frontiersman Someone who lives in the area between settled and unsettled land

gunnery The study and use of heavy guns; also the collection of guns and cannons on a ship

impress To force people to serve as sailors or soldiers

inauguration A ceremony held to mark the beginning of someone's term in office

Loyalist An American who stayed loyal or friendly to Britain

massacre To brutally kill many people

merchant Someone who earns money by trading or selling items

militia An army of private citizens organized to defend their country

morale The confidence and positive feelings of a group of people at a certain time

mortally Describing something that causes death

national anthem A song of loyalty to one's country

navy A country's military sea force, including ships and people

neutral Choosing not to fight on either side of a war

outpost A small military camp away from the main army which is used to guard against surprise attacks

Patriot A colonist who fought against British control in the American Revolutionary War

patriotic Showing love and support for one's country

peace treaty An agreement that officially ends a war

plunder To steal goods using force in times of war

port A town or city by the water where ships load and unload goods

privateer A citizen hired by the government to capture enemy merchant ships during war; also the ship used by a privateer

ragtag Something that is made up of mixed or different parts

recruit To convince someone to join the army or navy

representative Someone who acts or speaks for people as laws are made

restraint Showing self-control over one's actions

shipyard A place where ships are built and repaired

skirmish A fight between small parts of armies or fleets

sniper A hidden shooter who is skilled at hitting targets from far away

squadron A group of warships under the command of an officer

strategist A person who is skilled in planning action, especially in war

systematically Doing something in a planned, orderly way

territory In the United States, an area that is not yet a state

treacherous Something that has hidden dangers

treaty Written agreement between two countries, usually to prevent or end a war

tyrant A cruel and unreasonable leader

volunteer Offer to do a job instead of being commanded to do it

CHRONOLOGY

1763
Great Britain wins the Seven Years' War and takes over France's land in North America, including colonies in Canada.

1783
The 13 original colonies win the American Revolutionary War, ending British rule and creating the United States.

1799
Napoleon Bonaparte becomes the leader of France and has ambitions of expanding his empire in Europe. This brings France into conflict again with Great Britain.

1803
The United States buys Louisiana from France and doubles in size.

1807
Great Britain bans neutral countries from trading with France.
France and Britain blockade each other's ports.
The United States passes the Embargo Act banning U.S. trade with other countries.

1809
The United States replaces the Embargo Act with an act banning U.S. trade with Britain and France until they stop their interference.

1812
June 18 President Madison declares war on Britain and its colonies.
July 12 William Hull leads the first attack on Canada but soon retreats.
August 16 Brock and Tecumseh win an unlikely victory at Fort Detroit.

August 19 Isaac Hull captures and burns the H.M.S. *Guerriere*.
October 13 The British—with the help of Brant—win the Battle of Queenston Heights. Brock is killed.
October 25 Decatur captures the H.M.S. *Macedonian*.

1813
June 1 Broke captures Lawrence's ship, the U.S.S. *Chesapeake*.
June 22 Secord warns the British of a surprise attack on Beaver Dams.
September 10 Perry defeats Barclay at the Battle of Lake Erie.
October 26 De Salaberry and Macdonell successfully preventing an American attack on Montreal at the Battle of Chateauguay.

1814
March 27 Jackson wipes out Weatherford's "Red Stick" Creeks.
July 25 Drummond and Brown fight the bloody Battle of Lundy's Lane.
August 24 Barney fails to defend Bladensburg against Ross and Cockburn. Dolley Madison rescues national treasures before the British burn Washington.
September 11 Macdonough defeats the British at Plattsburgh.
September 13 Cochrane attacks Fort McHenry. Armistead refuses to surrender. The next day, Key sees Pickersgill's flag and writes the words to "The Star-Spangled Banner."

1815
January 8 Pakenham attacks New Orleans and is crushed by Jackson's army.

MORE INFORMATION

Books

Bozonelis, Helen Koutras. *Primary Source Accounts of the War of 1812*. Berkeley Heights, NJ: MyReportLinks.com Books, 2006.

Crump, Jennifer. *The War of 1812: Heroes of a Great Canadian Victory*. Canmore, Alta: Altitude Pub. Canada, 2007.

Mulhall, Jill K. *The War of 1812*. Huntington Beach, Calif: Teacher Created Materials, 2005.

Wallenfeldt, Jeffrey H. *The American Revolutionary War and the War of 1812: People, Politics, and Power*. New York, NY: Britannica Educational Pub. in association with Rosen Educational Services, 2010.

DVDs

History Channel Presents: The War of 1812 DVD Set This two-disc collection covers the involvement and achievements of the United States in the war.

War of 1812 This four-part documentary series from the National Film Board of Canada provides a Canadian perspective on the war.

WEBSITES

1812 History
http://1812history.com/

Archives of Ontario: The War of 1812 Exhibit
www.archives.gov.on.ca/english/on-line-exhibits/1812/index.aspx

Dictionary of Canadian Biography Online
www.biographi.ca/index-e.html?PHPSESSID=2fajfd42kemi34etuubvqujup5

Founders of America
www.foundersofamerica.org/index.html

Naval History and Heritage Command
www.history.navy.mil/index.html

The War of 1812 website
http://warof1812.ca

BIBLIOGRAPHY

The following books and web sites were used as the major sources of primary evidence included in this book:

Historical Narratives of Early Canada: http://www.uppercanadahistory.ca/brock/brock4.html

Conlin, Joseph R. *The American Past: A Survey of American History*. Cengage Learning, 2009.

The White House web site: http://www.whitehouse.gov/about/presidents/

Crump, Jennifer. *The War of 1812: Heroes of a Great Canadian Victory*. Altitude Publishing Canada Ltd., 2007.

Suthren, Victor. *The War of 1812*. Toronto: McClelland & Stewart Inc., 1999.

Dictionary of Canadian Biography Online:
http://www.biographi.ca/009004-119.01-e.php?BioId=36410

The Archives of Ontario: http://www.archives.gov.on.ca/english/on-line-exhibits/1812/detroit-victory.aspx

Excerpt from an account of the Battle of Queenston Heights:
http://www.warof1812.ca/queenstn.htm

Ohio Historical Society: http://www.ohiohistory.org/onlinedoc/war1812/lake_erie/0036.cfm

The Encyclopedia of Arkansas History and Culture:
http://www.encyclopediaofarkansas.net/encyclopedia/entry-detail.aspx?entryID=2872

America's Historic Lakes: The Lake Champlain and Lake George Historical Site:
http://www.historiclakes.org/Plattsburg/macdonough_letter.html

Naval History and Heritage Command:
http://www.history.navy.mil/trivia/trivia02.htm
http://www.history.navy.mil/bios/hull_isaac.htm
http://www.history.navy.mil/library/online/burning_washington.htm

Founders of America: http://www.foundersofamerica.org/decatur.html

Royal Navy web site:
http://www.royalnavy.mod.uk/history/ships/hms-shannon-1806/index.htm

Dolley Payne Todd Madison: http://rotunda.upress.virginia.edu/dmde/DPM0469

Rediscover 1812 web site: http://rediscover1812.com/?p=159

The Smithsonian: http://americanhistory.si.edu/starspangledbanner/

Maryland Women's Hall of Fame: http://www.msa.md.gov/msa/educ/exhibits/womenshall/html/pickersgill.html

The Naval War of 1812 by Theodore Roosevelt: http://www.gutenberg.org/catalog/world/readfile?fk_files=1472982&pageno=217

Remini, Robert Vincent. *The Battle of New Orleans: Andrew Jackson and America's First Military Victory*. Penguin, 1999.

Borneman, Walter R. *1812: The War that Forged a Nation*. New York: HarperCollins, 2004.

Hickey, Donald R. *Don't Give Up the Ship: Myths of the War of 1812*. Champaign, IL: University of Illinois Press, 2006.

INDEX